Work
for My

D1466859

YOUR KIDS AND MINE

Tana Reiff

AGS®

American Guidance Service, Inc.
Circle Pines, Minnesota 55014-1796
1-800-328-2560

Working for Myself

Beauty and the Business
Clean as a Whistle
Cooking for a Crowd
Crafting a Business
The Flower Man
The Green Team
Handy All Around
Other People's Pets
You Call, We Haul

Cover Illustration: James Balkovek
Cover Design: Ina McInnis
Text Designer: Diann Abbott

Printed in the United States of America
ISBN 0-7854-1115-1 (Previously ISBN 1-56103-901-2)
Product Number 40829
A 0 9 8 7 6 5 4 3 2

CONTENTS

Chapter

CHAPTER 1

Making a Big Change

Vanessa rocked baby Jarrod as she fed him. She remembered being rocked on her grandmother's lap in this same noisy chair. She would never fix the squeak. The sound was too sweet.

Vanessa hummed softly to herself. When the baby looked up and smiled, she was sure that she had never been so happy in her life.

But then she thought of going back to

work. Her leave of absence would be over in a week. Then she'd have to drop off Jarrod at the day-care center each morning. She knew she would think about him all day. As she looked down at Jarrod, a tear ran down her cheek. "How can I leave you?" she whispered.

That night she told her husband Reggie what she was feeling. "I've been thinking," she began. "Maybe I don't *have* to go back to work."

"I wish you didn't, honey," Reggie said. "But you know that we need two paychecks. What in the world are you talking about?"

"I'm talking about working at home," Vanessa said. "I'm talking about taking care of other people's children. You know—day care."

"*Here?* I don't know," Reggie said.

"I know there would have to be some changes," Vanessa said. "But think about it. My job didn't pay that much money anyway. And now we'll also have to pay for Jarrod's day care. I bet I could make just as much right here at home—maybe even more."

"I don't know if I want my house crawling with kids," Reggie said.

"It would only be during the day," Vanessa said, laughing.

"We'd better think about this real hard," said Reggie.

The next day Vanessa telephoned her friend Diana. Diana had been doing day care in her home for a couple of years now. Vanessa wanted to ask her some questions.

"I won't say it's easy," said Diana. "But I can't see myself doing anything else. I love kids, and I love being home. For me, it's a natural. Why don't you stop by and see for yourself?"

So the very next morning Vanessa packed up baby Jarrod and went over to Diana's house. As they walked inside, a flying doll hit Vanessa in the arm. Two little boys were eating their morning snack at the table. One of them had spilled his juice all over the floor. A baby was trying to climb the stairs. Two bigger children were punching each other. Another child was crying her eyes out. The TV was turned up so loud that it almost drowned out the children's noise.

"You *enjoy* this?" Vanessa asked her friend.

"I'm used to it!" laughed Diana. "You'd get used to it, too."

"You seem to have an awful lot of kids here," Vanessa said.

"I'm a few children over what I'm supposed to have," said Diana. "But so far I'm getting away with it. It's two extra checks, you know?"

Vanessa tried to talk more with Diana. But there was just too much going on around them. It was time for Vanessa and Jarrod to leave.

On the way home Vanessa saw a sign on a house. It said *Mrs. Carter's Day Care*. Vanessa walked right up and knocked on the door.

When an older woman answered, Vanessa told her why she had stopped by. "Come in and look around," the woman said. Vanessa and Jarrod went inside. Two babies and three toddlers were playing quietly on the floor. Soft music came from the radio. The TV was turned off.

Mrs. Carter showed Vanessa all around. When two of the children began fighting over a toy, the woman didn't get upset. Instead she calmly helped them work things out. Then she and Vanessa sat down together for a cup of coffee.

"Here's the way I look at it," Mrs. Carter began. "There's day care and then there's day care. If you want to, you can run a zoo. *Or* you can make a nice place for children to be. You just have to plan a little bit. And of course, you have to be ready for anything. All kinds of things happen along the way!"

"What else does it take besides good

planning?" Vanessa asked.

"It takes a certain kind of person," said Mrs. Carter. "You should be in good health and have plenty of energy. Does that sound like you?"

"Yes."

"You have to be able to keep your cool—no matter what."

"I do that pretty well."

"You have to really enjoy being with children. Day care takes up most of your waking hours."

"I understand that."

"You must have lots and lots of patience. And you must love children for what they are."

"Oh, yes."

"You must be able to keep the kids under control—but in a kind way."

"I learned about that when I worked in a summer camp."

"And it helps a lot to be a good problem solver."

"I really am," said Vanessa.

"One more thing. Don't expect to get rich at this kind of work."

"Oh, I don't," Vanessa smiled.

"Then, my dear, you just might have what it takes," Mrs. Carter said.

"Do you really think so?"

"Sure, I do. Now all you need to get started is a license."

A license? Vanessa hadn't thought about that. As soon as she and Jarrod got home, she put him down for his nap. Then she called the telephone number Mrs. Carter had given her. She wanted to find out how to get a day-care license.

CHAPTER 2

Dealing with Problems

Reggie got home late that night. Vanessa was so excited she couldn't stop talking. "I want to take care of kids in our home," she told him. "I called the city information service. They said there's a big need for family day care around here. They're sending me a state form to get a license. I have to take a child-care class and a first-aid course. They even told me about a family day-care group I can join."

"It sounds as if you really want to do this," Reggie said.

"I really do," said Vanessa. "But it has to be OK with you."

Reggie was quiet for a minute. Then he said, "Honey, I have to ask you something. Why do you *really* want to do this? Is it because you want to stay home with the baby? Or do you truly want to watch other people's kids?"

"Both," Vanessa answered. "Doing day care *does* let me stay home with Jarrod. But it's also a great way to make money by doing something I like to do. There's a lot more to day care than babysitting, you know."

"Then go ahead," said Reggie. "Get your license and do it. But not forever. Let's say that you'll do it until you feel ready to hold an outside job again. Or let's say you'll do it for two years— whichever comes first. Deal?"

"Deal."

The next morning Vanessa called her

old boss. She told him that she wouldn't be returning to work. Next, she called the day-care center. She told them that Jarrod wouldn't be going there after all.

Then the mail came. Vanessa tore open the fat yellow envelope from the city information service. Inside was a small pink book of laws about family day care. There was also a long list of questions.

Do you have a fenced-in yard?

Do you have a fire extinguisher in the kitchen?

Is there a smoke alarm on each floor of your home?

Are the floors and walls clean?

Do you have first-aid items on hand?

There were quite a few questions about Vanessa's health. There were questions about the play area and the kitchen. There were questions about heat, air, and bathrooms.

The list of questions went on and on. Altogether there were more than 60 questions on the list.

Then there was the state form. It had many boxes to be filled in. When she wasn't holding Jarrod, Vanessa worked on the form. It took her all day—and she still wasn't done.

She couldn't answer every question on the form. She wasn't sure if her house met the rules in every way. So she made a few more phone calls. She asked for a fire inspector to come and check out the house.

"You need a new screen on the back window," he said. "And you should get a new cover for your kitchen light. You'd better check out the zoning for this neighborhood, too."

Vanessa wrote down everything the inspector told her.

The fire inspector didn't like the looks of the upstairs smoke alarm. "You can get a new one for just a few dollars," he said to her.

Vanessa wrote that down, too.

Next the zoning inspector came out. The woman was still standing on the front porch when she said, "You can't have day care here."

"Why, what do you mean?" Vanessa cried out in surprise.

The zoning inspector pointed up and down the block. "No in-home businesses are allowed in this part of town," she said. "Businesses may be set up only in certain areas. This isn't one of them."

"But I was told there's a great need for child care in this area," Vanessa said. "Why won't the city let people use their homes to take care of children?"

"I'm not the one who makes the laws," the inspector said. "My job is to make sure they're obeyed."

"Are you telling me that there's no way I can get a day-care license?"

"No, I'm not," said the inspector. "You can take your case to the zoning board. If it's all right with them and your neighbors, the board may give you a *variance.* That means they decide that you are a special case. You know—they make an exception."

Vanessa's heart sank. She couldn't picture herself going before the zoning board. To her, it sounded like going to court to beg for mercy.

The zoning inspector saw how upset Vanessa looked. "Hey, it's worth a try," the woman said. "I'll even give you a tip. Before you go, join the family day-care group here in town. They can help you with the zoning board."

"Thanks," Vanessa said. She smiled and said good-bye to the woman. But inside she felt terrible.

Vanessa was still upset when Reggie got home from work. "What if I go to the zoning board and they turn me down?" she said. "Is it worth all this trouble? Maybe I should call my boss and ask for my job back. Maybe this day care idea isn't going to work."

"You told Mrs. Carter you were a good

problem-solver, right?"

"I did, didn't I?"

"Then prove it," Reggie said. "If you really want to do day care, you have to go for it. That means be willing to deal with problems."

Vanessa was tired. It had been a long day. She rocked Jarrod and put him to bed. Then she went to sleep herself. Jarrod woke up only once that night, so Vanessa got a pretty good night's sleep. The next morning, the sun was shining. She felt ready to face a new day.

CHAPTER 3

Zoning and Insurance

Vanessa put up a notice in her front window. Everyone who went by could read it. The notice stated very clearly what Vanessa planned to do. It said that she wanted a zoning variance to run day care in her home.

The zoning board meeting was a month away. Anyone in the neighborhood who didn't like Vanessa's plan could attend the meeting. Of course, Vanessa hoped that none of her neighbors would show up for the meeting.

The next day she heard talk in the neighborhood. Mr. Bright down the street was against her plan. He was telling people that a day-care home would be bad for the neighborhood. He was asking all the neighbors to come to the zoning board meeting. There they could all speak out against Vanessa's plan.

Vanessa joined the day-care group. Three of the members helped her get ready for the zoning meeting. They helped her prepare answers to the questions she might be asked.

Over that next month, Vanessa looked into other matters. She read that she should carry extra insurance for day care. So she got in touch with her insurance agent.

"You will need liability and accident insurance," the agent said. "Suppose a child falls and gets hurt. Suppose that happens because of something that you did or didn't do. Suppose the child falls because of a loose floor board. You need insurance to cover such things."

"I see," said Vanessa.

"But there's just one problem," the agent added. "If you have day care in your house, we'll have to drop your home insurance."

That night, Reggie said, "We can't drop our home insurance! But there might be some other way to work it out. The day-care group is helping you with the zoning problem. Maybe they can help with insurance, too."

The next morning Vanessa called Joanne from the day-care group. "Our local group is part of a big, national group," Joanne told her. "You're not the only one with insurance problems. The national group can help you get a rider for your home insurance."

"I don't know very much about insurance," Vanessa said. "What's a rider? Can you explain it to me?"

"First you need to find an insurance company that won't drop you for having day care," Joanne explained. "The rider is extra coverage on top of that home insurance. It will cover you for liability and accidents."

So Vanessa talked to the insurance agent again. Then she talked to the national day-care group. If she could get the zoning variance, the insurance would work out.

"Now all I have to do is face the zoning board," Vanessa told Reggie.

"You'll do OK," Reggie said. "After all, you have me and Joanne and the group behind you!"

Vanessa gave her husband a big hug. "You're the best," she said. "If we get past this zoning thing, I'm going to take you out to dinner!"

The night of the meeting, Reggie stayed home with Jarrod. Vanessa met Joanne and the others at City Hall.

"I'm scared," Vanessa told Joanne. "Suppose they *don't* give me a variance. Then all my work up to now will have been wasted."

Joanne smiled and put her arm around Vanessa. "Don't worry," she said. "You know what to say. You'll be just fine."

The meeting got started. After going through some other business, the man in charge turned to Vanessa. "So you'd like to have day care in your home," he said. "You live in an R-1 part of town. Why should we allow you a variance to run a business in your home?"

"Well, it's nothing like a store," answered Vanessa. "People will not be coming and going all day. Parking will not be a problem."

"It's still a business," said the man.

"But there is a real *need* for good child care in our area," Vanessa went on. "I would be doing the community a valuable service."

Then it was Mr. Bright's turn to speak.

"We don't want a crowd of little kids running all over the block," he said. "It's a quiet neighborhood now. A lot of senior citizens live there."

"The children would stay in my home or on the sidewalks at all times," Vanessa said. "They will not set foot on anyone's grounds. I will see to that."

Vanessa had a good answer ready for every question. Finally the board members took a few minutes to talk among themselves.

At last the man in charge turned back to Vanessa. "We have decided that you may have the variance. You may run day care in your home. However, all of the children must go home by 6 p.m. And you may not take children on Saturdays and Sundays. Do you agree to that?"

Vanessa could hardly keep from jumping up and down. "Yes," she said, smiling ear to ear.

"Very well," said the man. "You may sign the papers as you leave."

Vanessa signed the papers. Then she and Joanne and the others left the meeting. Outside Vanessa *did* jump up and down. She hugged the woman from the day-care group over and over. "I can't thank you enough!" she cried.

"You did it yourself," Joanne said. "We just helped you get ready."

"I told my husband I'd take him out to dinner tomorrow night," Vanessa said. "Why don't the three of you come along to help us celebrate?"

"I have a better idea," Joanne said. "You two go and I'll watch Jarrod."

"Do you mean it? Wow! Thanks!" said Vanessa. "That's great!"

Vanessa was still smiling the next night at dinner. She and Reggie went to their favorite restaurant. It was the first time they had been out together since Jarrod was born. After they finished dinner, they talked about the future. They had a wonderful time.

CHAPTER 4

Making Plans

One afternoon about two weeks later, Vanessa opened the mail. The state license had arrived! So had the forms for the food program the day-care group had told her about. Vanessa would need to keep good records of what she fed the children. Then the government program would pay her back.

Vanessa sat back in the chair. "This is starting to seem real," she said to herself.

"Do I really want to go through with it? Do I really want to spend ten hours a day with little kids who aren't mine? Can I really make their day happy and busy?"

She held the license in her hand. She read her name on it one more time. "Yes," she said. "I'm good with kids. I really want to do this."

Vanessa had much more to think about. How much money would she need to get her business started? How much would the business cost for the whole first year? There were lots of things she had to do. She had to sign up for child-care and first-aid classes. And, of course, she had to find children to take care of.

"Whaaaaaah!" came Jarrod's cry from upstairs.

"But all that has to wait for now," she thought. She ran up to get the baby. She couldn't believe that his nap time was over already. All she had done was read the state papers.

Vanessa fed Jarrod and put him on a

blanket on the floor. He lay on his back and kicked his little feet in the air. He smiled as he watched the ceiling fan go round and round.

"How do you feel about having some friends over every day?" Vanessa asked him. "Would you like that? Yes? Not another baby, you say? You say that you're my only baby? Well, OK."

Baby Jarrod kicked his feet like crazy. He liked it when his mother talked to him in a sweet, calm voice.

"Let's see if we can get some older children to come here for day care," said Vanessa. "How about a two-year-old, a three-year-old, and a four-year-old? Maybe one more. We'll see. Mommy doesn't want too many little ones who are still in diapers. Oh, my, no!"

Vanessa kept on talking to Jarrod as she got out a paper and pencil. She made a list of everything she needed to spend money on. Some toys and a little table. School fees for the two classes. New window screens. New light cover. New smoke alarm. Paper and crayons. Extra toilet paper. Booster seats. Extra sheets and blankets. She added up everything. That was the amount she would need for a start-up budget.

Then Vanessa wrote down what she would have to pay for during the next year. Insurance. Cleaning supplies. Day-care group membership. She added up everything. That was the yearly budget.

All of a sudden Jarrod began to cry. "What's the matter?" Vanessa asked as she picked him up. "Oh, sure. Wet diaper. Can't have that, can we?"

She changed his diaper. Then she figured out how much she needed to charge to take care of each child. In no time at all, it was time to make dinner.

Vanessa got out her pencil and paper again the next morning. She worked out a daily plan of activities for the children. First there would be a morning song. Then art time. Then music time. Then snack. Then free play. Then lunch. And so on.

As she worked, Vanessa noticed that Jarrod wasn't very happy today. He began to cry and cry. Vanessa rocked him in the squeaky chair, but he was still upset. There was a strange look in his eyes. He felt warm. This baby was sick.

Vanessa called the doctor's office. "I guess I'd better take a look at him," the doctor said. "Can you come in right away?"

Reggie had driven the car to work. So Vanessa went next door. She hoped that her neighbor Sally could drive them to the doctor's.

"What if this happens when I have a house full of kids?" Vanessa said to Sally. "What will I do?"

"I can help you out anytime," said Sally. "I'll drive you, or I'll watch the kids and you can take my car."

"That's so good to know," Vanessa said to Sally. "I hope I won't need you very often, but I'm glad you're here."

"No problem," Sally said. "I'm almost always at home."

The doctor said that Jarrod had an infection in his ears. It wasn't the first time, and it wouldn't be the last. As usual, the doctor gave Vanessa an order for some medicine. She started giving it to him right away. Jarrod was better by that evening.

That evening Vanessa and Reggie relaxed. Reggie was watching TV. Vanessa was thinking about sick children. Her own sick child was one thing. But what if a day-care child got sick? Would she take a sick child? She began to write down some rules. Every parent would get a copy of the list.

CHAPTER 5

Setting Up

The next day was Saturday. That was yard sale day in the neighborhood. "Wake up, little guy!" Vanessa said as she kissed Jarrod awake. "We're going on a shopping trip!"

Vanessa dressed the baby and put him in his stroller. She cut out the list of yard sales from the newspaper. Then she took the list of things she needed for day care. She grabbed a big shopping bag, and off they went out the door.

"The early bird gets the worm!" she told Jarrod. "Let's find us some good, juicy worms this morning!"

Vanessa found some toys at a yard sale just down the street. They looked almost new. She bought five toys and spent only four dollars. She tucked the toys into the back of the stroller.

Over on the next block she found some nice, old blankets. She bought six for ten dollars. She folded them up and laid them on the stroller roof.

Across that street Vanessa found a set of blocks and a pile of picture books. She bought all of them for five dollars. She was especially happy to find a little red table and chairs—the whole set for ten dollars!

Two blocks away she found riding toys, puzzles, and games. The puzzles and games fit in her shopping bag. She told the people she would come back with a car for the bigger things.

Vanessa had left the house with $30.00. She came home with just $2.00. "Not bad," she said to herself. "I got a lot for my money today."

The same day, she began to save all kinds of things. She stopped throwing away plastic food trays and egg cartons. The children could make craft projects out of them. She kept old clothes for dress-ups. She started a pile of old magazines so the children could cut out pictures. And she covered shoe boxes for the children to keep their things in.

Vanessa made a reading corner in the dining room. There she piled up some old pillows next to a small bookcase. The corner was small, but it was very cozy.

The next day she drove Reggie to work. Then she and Jarrod headed for the discount market. There she bought cases of canned goods and snack foods. She also bought a giant box of crayons.

Vanessa felt ready. She put her name on the list of day-care homes at the city information service. She made a big sign for her front window. She put holiday lights all around the sign. Anyone walking by could see it.

Parents began calling or stopping in right away. Most of them said they were checking out places for their children. Many said they were having trouble finding a good home.

Vanessa showed the parents and small children around. She talked with each of them for a few minutes. She also gave them a list of references. These were people who had known Vanessa for a long time. They would speak well of her when the parents called to check her out.

Vanessa decided which children she would take. She called their parents. "I want you to understand two things," she told each parent. "First, I'll try each child for two weeks. If things aren't working out by then, you'll have to find other day care. And, second, you should know that I plan to return to work in no more than two years if everything works out."

Once everything was understood, Vanessa signed up four children. There would be one two-year-old, one three-year-old, and one four-year-old. The two-year-old and the four-year-old were brother and sister. That meant that Vanessa would only have to deal with two sets of parents.

Vanessa had one more thing to do before the children came. She did a safety check. She got down on her hands and knees, just like a small child. Then she crawled all around the house, looking for trouble.

Was there anything within reach that could break? Yes. Vanessa moved the bowl her grandmother had given her. Was there enough light on the stairway? Yes. She could see to the top of the stairs without any trouble.

Were there safety locks on all the cupboard doors? There were. Reggie thought they were a pain, but they had to be there for the children's sake.

Were toys kept on a shelf instead of a toy box? Yes. No one in this house was going to get hit on the head with a toy-box lid.

Were there any places on the floor that someone could slip and fall? Vanessa felt all around the floors. She laid a rubber mat in front of the kitchen sink.

At last she was sure that the house was safe for kids.

The next morning at 8:00 A.M. the doorbell rang. Vanessa's first day care child came inside. It was the three-year-old. Her name was Chrissy. She held a teddy bear in one hand. Her other hand was locked around her mother's leg.

CHAPTER 6

The First Day

Vanessa looked at Chrissy. She was glad she had gone to the child-care class. She had learned what to do with a child who was afraid to leave her parent.

Chrissy started to cry.

"Tell her that you'll be back at 5:00," Vanessa told Chrissy's mother. Then she gently pulled Chrissy from her mother's leg. She picked up the unhappy little girl. "Go ahead and say good-bye," Vanessa told the little girl's mother.

Chrissy was really screaming now. Vanessa sat down and cuddled the child in her lap.

"She'll be all right," Vanessa said to the mother. "Just say a nice good-bye and don't look back." She rocked Chrissy back and forth in her arms.

The mother looked ready to cry, too. "Remember, honey, I love you," she told Chrissy. Then she closed the door behind her and went on to work.

Vanessa was glad that Chrissy was the only new child today. This could prove to be a long nine hours. But a minute or so after the mother left, Chrissy jumped off Vanessa's lap.

"Who's that?" Chrissy asked, pointing to Jarrod.

"That's Jarrod," Vanessa said. "Would you like to play with him?"

Chrissy lay down on her stomach. She looked at Jarrod eye to eye. Then she touched his face. Jarrod didn't like that.

He batted his hand at Chrissy. The surprised girl let out a cry. She hopped up and ran to Vanessa.

Vanessa held her again. "How would you like to sing a morning song?" Vanessa began to sing. She took Chrissy's hands and clapped them together. Pretty soon Chrissy was clapping and singing along.

Then Vanessa carried Chrissy over to the little red table. She laid out some paper and crayons. Chrissy sat on one of the little chairs. "I like to draw," she said in her squeaky little voice.

In no time at all, the paper was full of Chrissy's scribbles. "Well, aren't you hard at work!" Vanessa told her.

Chrissy made five drawings that morning. Vanessa taped them to the wall. She sat Jarrod in his baby seat in front of the drawings. He seemed to like the bright colors. He looked at them as if they were great art works.

Vanessa put on a music tape. She and

Chrissy danced all around the living room. After that Vanessa gave Chrissy some peanut butter crackers and milk. Then she put Jarrod in his crib for his morning nap.

Chrissy played with some toys. After lunch Vanessa read Chrissy and Jarrod a story in the cozy corner. Then Chrissy went in for her nap.

At 5:00 Chrissy's mother returned. "How did it go?" she asked Vanessa.

"It takes a little time for a child to get used to new day care," said Vanessa. "But Chrissy did very well."

"I'm so glad," the mother said. "I worried all day."

"We didn't have time to go over the paperwork this morning," said Vanessa. She gave Chrissy's mother some papers. "I need you to return these forms tomorrow. There's a contract to sign, a health record, and an emergency form. You should keep the list of rules."

"Rules?" the mother said. "Such as?"

"You have to call me if you'll be more than ten minutes late to pick up your child. The contract states the time you will drop off and pick up your child. It also says that you will pay me every other Friday. And you'll pay for two weeks of day care at a time."

"What happens if Chrissy is sick?" the mother asked.

"If it's just a little cold or stomach ache, she may come here," Vanessa said. "But if she has a fever, you won't be able to bring her."

The mother didn't look happy to hear that. "What will I do then? If I have to stay home with her, I'll lose a day's pay at work."

"I'm sorry," Vanessa said. "I don't have an extra room for sick children. I know that children will eventually catch whatever is going around—but I can't *ask* for trouble, can I?"

"I wish that you had told me about all your rules before I started Chrissy here," said the mother with a frown.

"I'm sorry," said Vanessa. "But the rules are for everyone's benefit—Chrissy's, too."

A few days later, the two-year-old and four-year-old children arrived. The two-year-old was named Michael. His four-year-old sister was Michelle. Vanessa went over the contract with their father right away.

Vanessa's house had become a busy place. She followed her plan each day. First there was a morning song. Then art time. Then music time. Then snack. After free play, the children had lunch. First thing in the afternoon was story time. Then nap time. Then snack time. Late afternoon was more free play. Sometimes they had a little lesson in using buttons and zippers instead of music. Sometimes, instead of free play, they went for a walk.

At least once a day, Vanessa had to look for Michael. Sometimes she found him under a bed. Sometimes he was out in the fenced yard. Almost always, the busy little boy was somewhere he wasn't supposed to be.

At the end of each and every day, Vanessa rocked Jarrod in Grandma's chair. Sometimes she was the first one to fall asleep.

CHAPTER 7

Adult Problems

"So how is it going?" Reggie asked Vanessa one night.

"Fine. Great," said Vanessa. "I feel like a wet dish rag at the end of the day. But I love the children."

"I wish you weren't so tired every night," Reggie said. "I'd like a little time with you, too."

"I'd be tired if I went out to a job," Vanessa said. "When I got home, I'd still have the baby to take care of."

"Well, *I* need some time, too," Reggie said. He paused for a moment. Then he said, "And I'm not so sure the kids are all fine, either."

"What do you mean?" Vanessa asked with a worried look on her face.

"I found a crushed peanut butter cracker next to our bed," said Reggie. "Those kids aren't supposed to be upstairs in our room."

"It must have been Michael," said Vanessa. "He goes all over the place. I'm always looking for him."

"Well, try to keep a better eye on him. Who knows what he'll get into next? It's your job to keep him from running wild."

"Excuse me," said Vanessa, with a flash of anger. "I have *four* children to watch. I have my hands full."

"I don't mean to pick on you," Reggie said. "But remember, this is our home, first. It may not be a palace, but it's what I come home to. Just try to keep the kids under control, all right?"

Vanessa was upset. But then she thought of the check she'd gotten that day from Michael and Michelle's dad. It was her first paycheck from her new business. It would feel great to take it to the bank. Chrissy's mom had forgotten to bring a check. She said she would bring it on Monday.

But on Monday, Chrissy's mom forgot again. She forgot on Tuesday, too. And she picked up Chrissy a half-hour late without bothering to call. On Wednesday she was late again and she still didn't bring a check. Vanessa told her that she'd need the money or she wouldn't be able to take care of Chrissy anymore.

On Thursday, Chrissy's mom was late, but she did bring a check. "I'm really sorry," she said. "By the way, my friend is looking for a new sitter for her little boy. Would you like to take on another day-care child?"

Vanessa thought about her talk with

Reggie. Maybe she shouldn't take another child. She didn't need another parent like Chrissy's mom, either. But the extra money would be nice. The state allowed her to keep up to six children. She decided to give it a try. She told Chrissy's mom that the friend and her son could stop by to talk.

The next day five-year-old Brandon and his mother came over. Vanessa liked the woman right away. She thought Brandon was very cute. The woman asked if Vanessa could pick up Brandon after kindergarten.

"I guess so," Vanessa said. "The school is only two blocks away. We can all walk over together." She said that she could start picking up Brandon on the next Monday.

On Monday at noon, it was time to pick up Brandon. But Jarrod was still down for his morning nap. He wasn't very happy when Vanessa woke him up. He cried all the way to the school.

Jarrod was asleep again Tuesday at the same time. Vanessa called Sally next door. "I need a little help," she said. "Can you wait here with Jarrod while we walk up to the school?"

"Sure," said Sally. In a couple of minutes she knocked on the door.

Sally said she'd be happy to come over anytime that Vanessa needed her help. Sally worked late afternoons and evenings. She said it was no problem at all to help Vanessa out.

A few days later Vanessa had to call Sally again. The phone rang and rang but there was no answer. She walked across the yard and knocked at the door. Sally wasn't home. Vanessa woke up Jarrod and went to pick up Brandon at school.

"I'm sorry," Sally told Vanessa later that day. "I got stuck in a long line at the market."

Over the next several days, the same thing kept happening. One day Sally was asleep. Another day she had to go to the doctor. Another day she had gone shopping with a friend. Vanessa had to give up on her. She knew that she wouldn't be able to count on Sally.

On top of that, Brandon was causing trouble. From his first day with Vanessa, he picked on the little kids. He always wanted his own way. He didn't seem to know what to do with himself while the other children napped. Vanessa had her hands full even before Brandon. Now things were even worse. Something had to change.

CHAPTER 8

Questions and Answers

"Remember what you said to the parents," Reggie said. "You promised to try each child for two weeks. You said if things didn't work out, they would have to find other day care."

"I *did* say that," Vanessa admitted. "But I would hate to make Brandon change day care again."

"Why do you suppose he had to change the last time?" Reggie asked. "I'll bet he got kicked out of the last place."

Vanessa hadn't thought of that.

"I say, give this kid two weeks," said Reggie. "That's fair. If he doesn't shape up by then—he's out."

Brandon didn't get any better. One day he walked across the room and hit Michael in the face.

"Why did you hit Michael?" Vanessa asked him.

"Because he was playing with my toy," said Brandon.

"We're not going to fight over toys," said Vanessa. "We're going to share. Now, go over and tell Michael that you're sorry."

Brandon's head was down. "I'm sorry," he whispered.

"Can you say it so that Michael can hear you?" said Vanessa. She lifted Brandon's chin so he could look at Michael's face.

"I'm sorry," said Brandon. Then he grabbed the toy from Michael's hand.

Vanessa took it away from him.

It took some time for Vanessa to help the boys work things out. She set the kitchen timer for five minutes. When the bell rang, Michael had to give the toy to Brandon. By that time, however, Brandon was interested in a different toy.

The next time Vanessa picked up Brandon at school, he didn't feel well. She could see that he was really sick. As soon as he got to her house, he threw up on the living room rug. Vanessa put him to bed and cleaned up the mess.

Vanessa called Brandon's mother at work. "I'm afraid that Brandon's sick. You'd better come and get him," she said. The mother came right over.

But then the mother said, "I hope we don't have to pay for today."

"You know that you pay by the week," said Vanessa.

"But that doesn't seem fair," Brandon's mother complained.

"I picked him up at school," said Vanessa. "I cleaned up his mess and put him to bed. Also, this is my *job*. I have to count on regular pay each week just like you do. And I must tell you—Brandon's been quite a problem."

The mother didn't see Vanessa's point of view. She said that Brandon was always a perfect angel at home.

Finally Vanessa gave in. "All right, I'll only charge you for the time that Brandon was here today."

Brandon's mother lifted him up. As she did, three pieces of red candy dropped from his pocket.

"What in the world is that?" the mother said. "Brandon's not supposed to have anything with red food coloring in it." She turned to Vanessa. "It makes him wild. And it can make him sick, too."

"Why wasn't it listed on Brandon's health form?" said Vanessa.

"It wasn't? Oh, dear! I thought I had listed it under *Other Allergies*," said

Brandon's mother.

Vanessa showed the woman the form. Red food coloring wasn't listed.

"I'm sorry. This is all my fault, Vanessa," the woman said.

"I want to go home," Brandon cried.

"First tell me where you got that red candy," his mother said.

"My friend at school gives them to me every day."

"I'll talk to the teacher," the mother said. "And from now on, please read the labels of anything you give him, Vanessa. Red food dyes are a no-no."

The candy at school stopped. And Vanessa stopped serving anything with red dye in it. Like magic, Brandon seemed to become like a new boy. The child stayed.

Vanessa found a helper through the senior citizens' club. She was a woman from the neighborhood. Every day she came over while Vanessa picked up Brandon. Mrs. York never missed a day.

And she usually stayed to help out with lunch. Vanessa wanted to pay her, but she wouldn't take any money. She said she was just happy to help. Sometimes she even watched Jarrod at night so Vanessa and Reggie could go out.

Chrissy's mom still showed up late most days. She always said that she had to work late. And she always said that she couldn't get to a phone. Every time she was late she had an excuse.

Vanessa started charging her a few more dollars for the extra time. But Chrissy's mother always took off the extra charge. And she always paid late. Vanessa knew that something would have to be done.

"I don't want to lose Chrissy," Vanessa told the mother. "She's a great kid. But there is problem here. It's not fair to ask me for extra time and not pay for it. And it's not fair for you to pay so late."

"At least I pay," said the mother.

But the checks got later and later.

When the payments fell six weeks behind, Vanessa told the mother not to bring Chrissy anymore. "It makes me very sad," she said. "I love your child. But I can't give her free day care. I'm trying to run a business. It's not fair to the parents who pay—*or* to me."

So Chrissy stopped coming. The house felt different without her. Vanessa missed her squeaky little voice. Even worse, Vanessa had to take Chrissy's mother to small claims court. The judge ordered the woman to pay up. Vanessa was glad she had the contract to back her up.

She called the city information service. "Please put my name back on the day-care list," she said. "I have an opening for one new child."

CHAPTER 9

Learning Everywhere

The new child was a three-year-old girl named Ashley. Vanessa found her easy to take care of. The little girl always had a smile. She listened to Vanessa. And she got along well with four-year-old Michelle. Vanessa hoped that someday she might have a little girl just like Ashley.

When Jarrod gave up his morning nap, Vanessa started taking the children out more. There were lots of places to go. Usually they went out while Brandon was in school. Jarrod, Michael, Michelle, and Ashley just loved the little field trips.

One morning they went to a park four blocks away. The children played on the big jungle gym. They ran up and down the grass and played in the big sandpile.

By the time they got home, they ate enough lunch to feed a young pony. Vanessa was glad that her helper was there. Mrs. York made eight peanut butter sandwiches for five children that day. She cut up four whole carrots. She poured a whole quart of milk. Vanessa made sure that she filled in the forms and got paid back for all that food.

There was also a pet store close by. Vanessa called and asked if the children could take a look around. The owner said it would be all right. A young man led the way. He showed the children a few of the pets. He let them watch him feed the puppies. He even let them hold the kittens and pet their soft fur.

"What was your favorite part of the pet store?" Vanessa asked them when they got home.

"The puppies!" said Michelle.

"No, the kittens!" said Ashley.

Another day Vanessa took the children to a fire station. More than once they went to watch a new house being built. Once a week they went to the library. And they never missed a play at Brandon's school.

The children learned many things at home, too. They worked on making their own peanut butter crackers. They played peek-a-boo with Jarrod. They learned how to use buttons and zippers. Vanessa loved to hear them say, "I did it myself!"

Every day Vanessa made sure the children had plenty of time just to play. She wanted them to learn to get along with each other. There was lots to learn from playing in a group.

Michelle and Ashley always brought

their own dolls to the house. They spent hours and hours pretending to be little mothers. Vanessa would laugh when she heard them saying things they had heard *her* say.

Michael missed Brandon in the mornings. He wanted to play with the girls, but he didn't have his own doll.

"We have some extra dolls here," said Vanessa. "Would you like to play with one?"

Michael took the doll and joined in with the girls. But he wasn't used to playing with a doll. He was a little rough with it. In no time at all, he came running to Vanessa. In one hand was the doll. In the other hand was the doll's leg.

"What's the matter?" Vanessa asked. "Have you got a problem?"

"Look! My doll broke her leg," Michael cried.

"Oh, that's too bad," said Vanessa. "Do you think we could fix her?"

"Maybe we should take her to the

hospital," Michael said.

Vanessa helped Michael dress up like a doctor. She got out some clean rags and helped him wrap the doll's leg. Then she helped Michael snap the leg back on.

"There!" said Vanessa. "Your dolly is as good as new!" She gave him a real bandage to put on the doll's leg.

Michael skipped off with the doll. He wanted to keep wearing his doctor clothes. Michelle and Ashley had been playing house. Now all three children wanted to play hospital.

Michael liked playing dolls with the girls. Mostly, though, he played with his trucks. One morning the girls and Michael were all playing with trucks. Everything was fine until Michael and Michelle wanted the same truck. Michelle grabbed it out of Michael's hands. When Michael tried to grab it back, she threw it. The truck sailed across the room. It hit the wall and crashed to the floor.

When Vanessa heard the noise, she jumped up to see what was wrong. The children were all crying. Even Jarrod crawled over to see what was going on.

"It's OK," Vanessa said, when she saw what had happened. She hugged the children and wiped their tears.

"Can we take the truck to the hospital?" Michael asked.

Vanessa looked at the truck. It was in pieces. It couldn't be fixed.

"I have an idea," she said. "Why don't we take the truck apart and see what's inside? Let's figure out how it was made."

So they took apart the rest of the truck, piece by piece. They looked at it inside out. Vanessa told them the names of all the parts. The children learned a lot from that broken truck.

After the children went home that evening, Vanessa threw the broken toy in the trash. The little toy truck had done its job.

C H A P T E R 10

A Big Surprise

Michelle and Ashley wore ladies' hats. They were pretending to be mothers. They dressed their babies and took them to the store. Michael ran the play store in the corner of the dining room. Michelle and Ashley put play food in their shopping carts. Michael took their play money. Then the two mothers went home and put their babies to bed.

Brandon was in first grade now. He

came to Vanessa's after school for an hour and a half. Today he and the new boy Kenny were holding a road race in the living room. Michael joined in now and then. But he was busy playing father for the babies, too.

Jarrod crawled from one busy child to the next. Mostly he watched them play. The girls wanted him to be their baby, but he kept crawling away.

Vanessa put on a music tape. She handed out fancy clothes from the dress-up box. The children marched to the music. It was a fine parade.

"This is all right," Vanessa said to herself. "I'm home with my child and earning money, too." Then she went back into the kitchen and made herself a cup of tea. She wasn't feeling very well today. Maybe the tea would settle her stomach.

It didn't. In five minutes she was in the bathroom, sick as a dog.

As it turned out, Vanessa was pregnant. It was another week before she found out for sure.

"I know we weren't planning this yet," she said to Reggie. "What do you think I should do? All these kids and their parents are depending on me. And I was only a few months away from going back to work. Now what?"

"Wait a few months," Reggie said. "You can think about it before you start showing. How do you feel about day care at this point?"

"Well, it's true that it's not a nine-to-five job," Vanessa said, laughing. "Oh my, no! My hours are more like seven to six! But I love it. I really do."

About two months later, they talked again about the future. Vanessa had decided what she wanted to do. And her plan was fine with Reggie.

The next afternoon, Ashley's mom came to pick up her daughter. Vanessa came to the door with one child on her hip and one at her feet.

Ashley's mom said, "You've got a nice

little thing going here, don't you?"

"Yes, I surely do," said Vanessa. She looked at the other children playing quietly on the floor. "These are wonderful children. I love having every one of them. And I'm so happy that I can stay home with Jarrod." She felt how heavy Jarrod was getting.

"Are you thinking about going back to work?" Ashley's mom asked. "It's been almost two years, hasn't it? What are your plans?" She had no idea that Vanessa was pregnant.

Vanessa thought it was a good time to talk. "I know I told everyone I would go back to an outside job in two years. I wanted you to know that you would have to find other day care. But the fact is— I'm pregnant again."

"My goodness," said Ashley's mom. "That changes things, doesn't it? What are you going to do?"

"I'm planning to work as long as I feel up to it," Vanessa said. "Then I'll take six months off with the new baby. After that I'll be ready to start up the day care again."

"Will you be taking any new babies?" Ashley's mom asked.

"Gee, I don't know," said Vanessa. "Jarrod might still be in diapers. With the new baby, that would make three in diapers. Why do you ask?"

"Well, the fact is, I'm pregnant, too!" said Ashley's mom. "But I can only take off three months from my job. I'll need day care when I have to go back to work."

"That's great!" said Vanessa. "You know how much I love Ashley. I always thought I'd like to have a daughter just like her. If your new baby is half as easy, I'd be happy to take her—*or* him!"

"Well, we think *you're* great, too, Vanessa," said Ashley's mom. "You've given our little girl so much. Your home is a wonderful place for a child to be. And you help the children learn so many important and helpful things."

"Thanks," said Vanessa.

"You'll be the first person we call for child care," the woman said. "We tell all our friends how lucky we are to have found you. We wouldn't even consider taking the new baby anywhere else!"

That night, like every other night, Vanessa rocked Jarrod in Grandma's old chair. The squeak was as loud and as sweet as ever. Some things should never change, Vanessa thought.

But some things *do* change. Jarrod was walking now. The house was full of happy children every day. Vanessa had found a good way of making a living. Her business bank account was in good shape. And a new baby was on the way.

More than ever, Vanessa was sure that children would always be a big part of her life. She could see herself doing day care at home for years to come. And who knows? Maybe someday, when her children grew up, they would rock their own babies in this very same old chair.